SCOTLAND IN COLOUR

SCOTLAND
in colour

Introduction and commentaries by
WILFRED TAYLOR

Photographs by
NOEL HABGOOD

B. T. BATSFORD LTD
London

Text filmset by Filmtype Services Limited, Scarborough,
Yorkshire
Printed and bound in Hong Kong by Leefung-Asco
for the publishers B. T. Batsford Ltd,
4 Fitzhardinge Street, London W1H0AH

First published 1973
Second Impression 1975
Third Impression 1978
ISBN 0 7134 0026 9

CONTENTS

Introduction

'On the whole, I must say I think the time we spent
there was six weeks of the densest *happiness I have*
met with in any part of my life; and the agreeable and
instructive society we found there in such plenty has
left so pleasing an impression on my memory that, did
not strong connexions draw me elsewhere, I believe
Scotland would be the country I should choose to spend
the remainder of my days in.'

Benjamin Franklin.

'But, Sir, let me tell you, the noblest prospect which
a Scotchman ever sees, is the high road that leads him
to England!'

Samuel Johnson.

The American, whose only title was the honorary doctorate conferred on him by St Andrews University, was more generous and endearing, in his valedictory to Scotland, than the Englishman, whose caustic gibe has lingered long in the annals of invective. The two celebrated sages were contemporaries and an interval of 14 years only separated their visits to Scotland, Franklin making his tour in 1759, and Johnson in 1773. It is one of my regrets that the two did not meet on Scottish soil.

Scotland can, and does, elicit contrasting responses from perceptive and discriminating travellers. In few other countries are the red and the blue poles of the emotional magnet so furiously energised. Although Franklin's charming affirmation is one of the prettiest compliments paid to Scotland by a pilgrim from abroad there is also more than a shred of truth in Johnson's cross-grained *aperçu*.

If the appeal of Scotland, to many of us who live and work in it, is irresistible, aspiration can also be deflected by discouragement. Far too many able, energetic, imaginative young Scots, for far too long, have followed Dr Johnson's advice and taken the high road that leads to England – not because the prospect was nobler, but because Scotland could not fulfil their expectations. Nor have they stopped short at England. The whole wide world has been their parish.

Many Scots who have participated in this vast hegira cherish a sentimental and a romantic passion for their homeland which can sometimes lead to manifestations so exuberant as to fill the native, stay-at-home Scot with wonder and even incredulity. I have found myself speculating, *in partibus infidelium*, on the occasion of St Andrew's Nights, or Burns Suppers, to which I had been privileged to be invited, if I myself really did toil and dwell in the country which released such cataracts of nostalgia and sentiment, which contributed the momentum for masquerades so exotic and so wondrous.

Sometimes, in the interests of national security and public safety, precautions have to be taken against excess of the *praefervidum ingenium Scotorum*. Once at a Burns supper in a town in the English midlands, my neighbour was a frail and kindly octogenarian ex-mayor. As the proceedings approached their frenetic and painfully unauthorised climax the poor old man became increasingly bewildered. When we were instructed to drink a mysterious, *ad hoc* toast with one foot on our chair and the other on the table the aged citizen, trembling in every limb, and evidently under the impression that if he did not comply some unspeakable Caledonian curse would plague his remaining years, was pathetically attempting to mount his chair. Gently pressing him back, while invocations in Lancashire Gaelic were thundering in all directions, I whispered, 'Let's sit this one out – it's a spurious emission.' It has never been my ambition to witness the sacrifice of an ex-mayor on the altar of tartan aggression.

Never have I seen such a stunning efflorescence of the clan ethos in all its polychromatic glory as at a St Andrew's Night dinner in Baltimore. Surrounded by the flower of the Commonwealth of Maryland, swathed in gorgeous plaids and studded with Cairngorm stones, I sat enchanted as the skirling of pipes announced the climax of the evening which was, I think, the rendering of 'Annie Laurie', by a tenor wearing a Glengarry with ribbons down to his waist. Above the din, as the spotlights whirled, one of my table-mates leaned over, and in a voice husky with emotion, uttered the words, 'All this must seem mighty tame and subdued to you, Mr Taylor, compared with what is taking place back home in Edinburgh.' I thought of the superb indifference with which my fellow citizens in Edinburgh would be responding to St Andrew's Night and scarcely felt the reassuring pat on the shoulder, intended, by my sympathetic neighbour, to console me for the half-hearted way they honoured our patron saint in sluggish Baltimore.

In even a brief sidelong glance at Scotland it is important to note the massive impact overseas of such a small country. Such, for instance, was the popularity of Walter Scott in the southern States of America that there were those who claimed that it was the romantic ideals which he propagated in his novels and poems which prompted the South to secede. If the diaspora sometimes, but not always, over-reacts extravagantly in parading its nostalgia one must not condemn entirely the enthusiasm. Behind the embarrassing gesticulation there is a real and deep sense of separation from the homeland, a homeland which lacked the resources, and possibly the imagination, to use the talents and energies of those emigré Scots. When I have been the guest of Scots abroad it has saddened me that, for historical and economic reasons, so much ability and so much vision should be lost to us at home.

But we who live in Scotland may, perhaps, be excused if we prefer Benjamin Franklin's affectionate eulogy to Samuel Johnson's rebarbative footnote. Discouragement and heavy unemployment there may be in Scotland and a restless desire to move to where the pastures are greener and the promises brighter, but, in a world in which the pressures intensify, Scotland is a wonderfully satisfactory country in which to live, a country which has not lost that kind of grace which Franklin found so captivating.

This book transmutes some of the external aspects of Scotland into pictures and few countries lend themselves so generously to pictorial presentation. There is a quality in the

14

northern light, sharp and utterly clear on the east coast, soft and caressing where the warmer winds blow in from the western seas, which can lend pure enchantment to city skyline as well as to vistas of mountain, moor, and loch. When, as in places like Morar, Achmelvich, Sandwood Bay, and the west coast of Harris, the ultramarine of the translucent water, the dazzling white of the beaches, and the emerald green of the machair fill the eye, the magical radiance overwhelms the senses: in an atmosphere fragrant with the aroma of peat one's thoughts dance to the rhythm of secret, wordless poems.

The effect of this natural beauty in boundless profusion can be psychological as well as physical. One heavenly, still, warm June evening I stepped out of the Sligachan hotel in the Isle of Skye. Faint lemon, green, and crimson streamers floated in a sky of pale, flushed blue, high above Sgurr nan Gillean, the rugged contours of which were mirrored in the calm, burnt-sienna water of a little lochan. To the south the fantastic, crenellated ridges of the Coolins reared up, like gigantic combers frozen forever over a backwash of heather. Time seemed to have melted into a blissful eternity.

By a little bridge, spanning a tawny burn, stood an elderly man, whom I at first took, from the strange, unflickering expression in his eyes, to be either blind or emotionally distressed. He was emotionally overcome, but not distressed. Quietly he turned to me and, in an English accent, said, 'I never knew there could be so much beauty.' He was paying his first visit to Scotland from his home in some Black Country town.

Outside the midland, industrial belt the loveliness of the Scottish landscape has largely escaped the clutch of commerce and the developer, although the discovery of vast quantities of oil under the North Sea is causing some anxiety among those who care for the face of Scotland. Little Holy Loch in Argyll may have been bedraggled and degraded by the savage, ungainly embrace of Polaris but, with isolated exceptions, the wilderness is too vast and too remote to yield readily to defilement. With the coming of the big hotel, tourist, and winter sporting complexes to the Spey valley, some of us selfishly thought that the Rothiemurchus fairy tale would be lost forever. But the Cairngorm country of forest, river, and loch, is more than big enough to absorb those profitable encroachments and, even if there has been some spoliation, the happy cries of children and ski-ers, of young people on adventure courses, proclaim that Scottish youth has discovered its heritage, a paradise too long denied to the children of the slums. With the imaginative establishment of attractive centres like Landmark, at Carrbridge, designed to open the eyes of city dwellers to the mysteries and enchantments of nature, a new era in open air education has begun.

To me the proof that Scotland's rich endowment of natural beauty can serenely resist almost any kind of vulgarisation may be cited in two words, 'Loch Lomond'. When one thinks of all the clichés and banalities, of all the atrocious doggerel and dismal ditties, of all the egregious flaneurs who have tried to lay this stretch of water under contribution, of all the marinas and caravan sites, of all the eleemosynary bag-pipers, of all the blasphemies and profanities committed in its name, Loch Lomond ought to have been drained of its beauty and reduced to the sorry status of a bog or morass.

Yet, every time I join the endless, internal combustion procession snaking along the western shore of this dreadfully insulted loch, on a sunny summer morning or evening, I come under the spell of the Ben, and of the green islands floating on the sparkling blue waters. More often than not my mind goes back to that improbable and quaint trio of English tourists, Dorothy and William Wordsworth and the exasperating, preposterous, ailing, lovable Samuel Taylor Coleridge.

The two poets and Dorothy met with a surly reception when they arrived at Luss, on the shores of Loch Lomond. At first the slovenly landlady at the inn was unwilling to provide them with accommodation for the night and to light a fire. As she tackled an unappetising meal Dorothy was depressed and compared the hovels of Luss unfavourably with the rose and honeysuckle embowered cottages of Somerset. She must have felt that the whole idea of a Scottish expedition had been a mistake.

But soon she cheered up. During their Scottish visit brother and sister, like Franklin, were to experience some of the happiest moments in their lives. On the way to Luss they had sighted, close to the shore, a little, wooded island, which had enraptured their vision. 'What a perfect place for William,' Dorothy reflected, with sisterly solicitude. When they were rowed across to the islet, Inchtavannich, it lived up to their

17

expectations. From then on the intrepid travellers were frequently in transports of delight over the scenery and the courtesy and dignity of the simple Highlanders who offered them hospitality. Later on not even the prospect of meeting Walter Scott deterred them from doubling back on their tracks so that they could re-visit Loch Lomond and the Trossachs.

I like to think of the abstracted, solemn William Wordsworth, absorbed in the contemplation of the scene, absent-mindedly dropping the bundle containing the party's provisions into the water, while transferring from one small boat to another on Loch Lomond. During that rewarding and lengthy journey in 1802 he seems to have been in great form. He even made a joke.

Sir Compton Mackenzie, that superb raconteur, nesophile, and man of standing, who, until his death at the age of almost 90, exerted his youthful spell over Edinburgh, would, on request, assume what he claimed to be a carefully studied rendering of William Wordsworth's accent and, in *oratio recta*, deliver what he believed to be the poet's only attempt at drollery. It was a hilarious performance, punctuated by deprecatory little sniggers as the bard approaches his punch line, a devastating retort to a simple inquiry from a farmer, near a stile somewhere in the Lake District. The witticism, when finally it exploded the suspense, would certainly have caused peals of merriment in any nursery.

Somewhere near Tarbet on Loch Lomond Dorothy and William set out to find a boatman's house. Although externally it was quite pretty the filthy interior shocked them. Dorothy humorously observed that it reminded her of the dwelling of a decayed weaver in the suburbs of a large town. But it was William who almost brought the house down. After a pause for meditation he merrily declared, 'It is quite Hottentotish."

Although Scots have been known to complain that their country does not get a proportionate return from its contribution to the UK exchequer Scotland, at least in some respects, comes rather well out of a partnership with England, cemented as recently as 1707. In terms of what is known as the Goschen formula, derived from a comparison of the respective populations of England and Scotland, the northern shareholder represents the unitary component in a 9:1 ratio.

Applying the Goschen formula to the one-inch Ordnance Survey maps, I have discovered that, in a total coverage of the UK, England rates 91 sheets, Scotland 78, and Wales 21. Instead of dominating by nine to one England, at least in the objective appraisal of the Ordnance Survey, enjoys a fractional lead only over Scotland. Scotland cannot reasonably protest that she has failed to secure an adequate place on the map. It would be imprudent to use the Goschen formula in predicting scores in international Rugby or Soccer games between England and Scotland.

The reason, of course, for Scotland's preferential treatment at the hands of the Ordnance Survey, is that, compared with England, she has an irregular coast line and is bountifully blessed with islands – to the tune of more than 700 – so that, when it comes to cartography, a much greater allowance must be made for water.

It can, one must admit in all honesty, rain in Scotland, but Scotland certainly does not regard her plentiful supply of rain water as an unmitigated curse. If at times what is euphemistically called a Scotch mist can mask the glories of the landscape that mere fact adds a quality of serendipity to the patriotic weather. The scenic beauty would lose its freshness if it were not, from time to time, and unpredictably, hosed down. And when it comes to distilling and blending no water in the world is superior to that found in Scotland: water has also proved its worth as the raw material for the North of Scotland Hydro-electric Board.

There are no visible sign-posts on what, as a roads scholar of some diligence, I take to be, under ideal conditions, the finest of all Scottish highways. This is the airway, Upper Red 38, which soars diagonally over the heart of Scotland, from Stornoway to Newcastle. It takes the pilots of Loftleidir, flying from Reykjavik to Luxembourg, about half an hour to cover the distance between the navigational beacons at Stornoway and Newcastle. Flying at over 30,000 feet they will span Scotland in about 25 minutes. Often when the sun is shining from a cloudless sky I glance up at the invisible UR 38 and envy those Icelanders whose regular job allows them to take in virtually the whole of the Scottish panorama at a glance.

Although when surveyed through the transparent hedge-rows of UR 38 Scotland might appear no more corrugated than a rumpled quilt adrift in a leafy pool it is essentially a land of high profile, in which it is natural to lift one's eyes to the hills. The broad, comfortable, parietal vistas and the level horizons, so familiar in much of England, are replaced by steep, green, bare hillsides when the Border is crossed. One looks in vain for a multitude of church steeples thrusting up from a plain. The hills and mountains tend to steal and to enclose the picture.

The high profile, sometimes combined with deep penetrations by the sea, is also responsible for an immense diversity within small compass, human as well as physical. This variety repeats itself in the speech patterns, the local dialects of the Scots. There is not only the sharp division between the lovely language of the Gaels, which bestows names sounding like reverberating organ chords on the mountains and lochs of the Highlands, and the various approximations of standard English spoken by the great majority of the population – there is also an astonishing variation in accent and idiom, so much so that inhabitants of communities only a few miles apart can be identified and localised phonetically.

The high profile also accounts for wide disparities in temper, attitude, and habit. The Borderer, for example, when he wishes to affirm his pride in the past, gets on a horse and rides the marches, after which he resorts to continuous revelry which can last, as in the Hawick Common Ridings, for three days without pause. The landed aristocracy plays little, if any, part in those annual exultations in the Debatable Lands.

The arrangements are otherwise when the Highlander finds himself in a mood to glorify his ancestry. For him it would be uncivilised to bestride a horse at about five or six o'clock in the morning and gallop round his croft or lazy beds. He prefers to attune his ear to the pipes in the intimate company of his family which, as with the Clan Cameron or the Clan Donnachaidh, may be represented by several hundred at a Clan Gathering. Although all clansmen are equal the Clan Chief is a person of invincible authority. Unlike the Borderer the Highlander respects the hierarchy, at least as far as owning fealty to his Chief is concerned. Although Clan Chiefs wear the kilt and lean on their cromags with inherited panache they have frequently been educated at English public schools and the modicum of Gaelic which they have dutifully assimilated can sometimes sound perceptibly Etonian to sensitive ears.

The Scot is essentially a romantic logician. In the past he excelled in metaphysics which, in the old Scottish universities, was rigorously separated from moral philosophy. At the heart of the Scottish ethos is a hard core of logic, embedded in a matrix of pure sentiment. The grid-iron rectangularity of the tartan is balanced by a gay profusion of colour. The precisely calculated geometry of the New Town of Edinburgh supports a poetry of masonry unique in these islands. The cool ration-ality of David Hume is matched by the tender sentiment of Robert Burns.

Ivor Brown once, as only a Scot could, wittily dismissed the history of his country as theology tempered by homicide. Theology may have lost most of its attraction in the Scotland of to-day but its spirit of lofty speculation is still preserved in the Scottish disposition to argument. England is seldom, among Englishmen, a subject for argument. Scotland is full of

Scots arguing about Scotland.

This propensity for dialectic accounts for the argumentative quality of much Scottish domestic architecture. There is a plain, solid, enduring appearance about most Scottish houses in sharp contrast to the mellow aspect of, for instance, the villages of the Cotswolds and West Suffolk. This comparative absence of ornamentation and extravagance, of splashes of colour, implies an implicit architectural recognition of the Argument by Design. Scottish homes are uncompromisingly designed to give adequate housing for inhabitants with weighty problems on their minds and a desire to settle burning issues.

Scottish architecture is seldom flighty, unless one associates that term with the old Scots term, 'to flite', which means to scold, wrangle, or argue. Although the high-riser now blots the urban sky-line Scottish cities still abound in the older tenement blocks in which dozens of families live in intimate proximity, sharing a common entrance or 'close', a word which, in Scotland evokes no echo of Anthony Trollope.

If the churches of Scotland, especially those housing congregations of the Free and Free Presbyterian denominations, are deficient in external and internal splendour, the prevailing greyness of stone can, it must be stated, be relieved by charming touches of colour. The red pantiled roofs, for instance, in the fishing villages of Fife present a gay, friendly appearance which would not discredit Cornwall. And many Scottish farm-houses and steadings merit the attention of the artist.

Scotland has an astonishing capacity for assimilating certain attributes from other countries. The influence of France, reflected in place names in Fife and West Lothian, and discerned in the lay-out of areas like the Grassmarket in Edinburgh and the centre of Kelso, reminds one of the Auld Alliance between the two countries. Edinburgh has to live with the reputation of being the Athens of the North, and when the strong boreal light plays on the gleaming granite façades of Aberdeen, the town of Bon Accord could be taken for a Baltic capital.

I confess to some surprise when a Prime Minister of the Netherlands once informed me that Edinburgh, with more hills inside its boundaries than Rome, reminded him strongly of the Hague. One hazy afternoon I was leaning on the battlements of Edinburgh castle, talking to a young American GI. 'It reminds me so much of my home town', he observed, taking in the vista with a sweeping gesture. 'And where is that?' I asked. 'Pittsburg', he murmured, dreamily. On another occasion I asked a Red Indian Chief called Rainbow Cloud, whom I had got to know slightly, if Edinburgh resembled in any way the place in which he had been born. Removing his pipe from his mouth he shook his head slowly from side to side 'No', he said, 'not like Boston.'

Scotland is a land of old battlefields and romantic castles, not all of them in ruins. Of all the inhabited castles Craigievaar, in Aberdeenshire, must be the most breath-taking. When first I glimpsed it its slender ginger-bread towers and turrets were shrouded in a silvery mist, making it seem like the *schloss* of some Hans Andersen princeling.

In a sketch of such short compass one can't do justice to Scotland's four largest cities. Since cities tend to rank themselves in terms of their academic furniture nowadays it may pass muster to treat them in this context. Edinburgh and Glasgow have two universities apiece. Long before it became prestigious to multiply urban groves of academe Aberdeen had two universities. It now has one, divided into two colleges, Marischal and King's. With its soaring, granite façade, Marischal dominates the centre of Aberdeen, a place of cool, impersonal splendour. Down the hill, in old Aberdeen, King's, with its fine chapel and handsome library, and the rosy little cathedral of St Makar's close by, makes Marischal appear a remote ineffectual don. There is a leisurely, warm, old world atmosphere, reminiscent of St Andrews University, about King's in its setting of green turf and gracious manses, in which dwell professors. The motto of the Earl Marischal, 'They have said – what say they? – let them say', intimately associated with the college bearing his name, resonant though it is, is too defiant for gentle King's. Aberdeen's university, like the University of Glasgow, and the University of St Andrews, had a churchman, Bishop Elphinston, as founder. Dundee's university was established less than 10 years ago by an Act of Parliament.

Scotland has a motley assembly of larger and smaller burghs, each of them worthy of survey in depth. It would be impossible within the scope of this introduction to generalise about their attractions, since they range all the way from, say, St Andrews, a veritable museum of Scottish history, to, for example,

Livingston, one of the half dozen new towns springing up in Central Scotland. St Andrews, that little jewel in a green setting by the North Sea, the town which rivalled Oxford in the affections of Andrew Lang, seems to be asleep and dreaming of the past. Livingston, springing up from the rather featureless, midland belt, in a countryside made theatrical at night by the flaming torches of the Grangemouth petroleum refineries, has no poet to celebrate its brand new streets. It keeps no pledges with the past, only promises with the future.

From the Rhinns of Galloway to Shetland, from Buchan Ness to the Isles of the Sea, the face of Scotland is infinitely explorable. Some of my own happiest journeys have been in quest of places so small and so elusive that they are indicated only by dots on large scale maps. There are three places named Gobernuisgeach on the maps. I have visited them all. The name derives from two Gaelic words meaning 'beak' and 'water'. Gobernuisgeach signifies the place of the confluence of waters, in foaming cascades. It was rough going to each of the places called Gobernuisgeach, but the sight of the rushing waters was entrancing. Speaking at a dinner in Winnipeg, one winter evening, I had the temerity to suggest that the Indian name of the Manitoban city, which has an enormous Scottish population and was founded by a Scot, the Earl of Selkirk, might be changed, out of respect to the two rivers, the Assiniboine and the Red River, which meet there, to Gobernuisgeach.

Some years ago I wrote about a dozen articles, vaguely intended to comprise a kind of parable on the beauty of the

26

Scottish landscape, headed, 'On Our Way to Wag'. Wag is no magnetic Mecca. It is a corruption of the Gaelic word meaning 'cave'.

My Wag, which I imagined as a kind of pot of gold at the end of the rainbow, and which lured me to travel hundreds of miles, is in the south-west of Caithness, a treeless county of endless horizons, vast, empty skies, brown peat moors, spectacular cliffs and archaeological sites. I had to get permission from a duke's factor to take the private track to Wag. A late September sunset was bathing one of my favourite mountains, Morven, in a flood of radiant light when, at last, I reached Wag, a mere nothing in a land of utter, ageless solitude. The only sound was the chuckle of a burn, a chuckle reaching a cadenza as, further down the strath, the water cataracted into a pool strewn with white boulders. Suddenly one stag after another peacefully silhouetted themselves on a dark ridge high above me, their antlers brilliantly etched on a flaming palette of gold, crimson, pale green, and orange. As they silently and majestically moved off into the darkling wilderness I turned homewards, down the green valley, a drive of 150 miles ahead of me, filled with a marvellous contentment of spirit.

It was a Scot, a strange, irascible, visionary Scot, Andrew Fletcher of Saltoun, who, in a letter written to the Marquis of Montrose and others, wrote the words, 'I knew a wise man so much of Sir Chr——'s sentiments that he believed if a man were permitted to make all the ballads, he need not care who should make the laws of a nation.'

Scotland has had ballad makers, *makars*, in plenty, to one of whom, at least, she annually pays tribute in a Niagara of impassioned rhetoric. But, possibly more than most countries, she holds her lawyers in much higher esteem. Her greatest living poet, with an international reputation, Hugh McDiarmid, lives in a two-roomed cottage, his regular source of income being a Civil List pension. He is a man of sensationally independent mind who is probably content to share the sentiment of his fourteenth-century predecessor, John Barbour, as expressed in perhaps the most moving declaration of freedom ever committed to verse:

> *A! Fredome is a noble thing!*
> *Fredome maiss man to have liking:*
> *Fredome all solace to man givis:*
> *He livis at ease that freely livis. . . .*

If the tone and temper of this preface to a portfolio of visual delight is lacking in *gravitas* it is because a Scot, when it comes to presenting the country in which he chooses to live, lacking the enviable detachment of an Alexis de Tocqueville, must be on his guard against undue solemnity. Like the hero in one of Rafael Sabatini's novels, who was 'born with the gift of laughter and a sense that the world was mad', one need not share the view that Scotland is so drenched in Presbyterian gloom that it is utterly deficient in *joie de vivre*.

But one must face the fact that there is a deep seriousness in the Scot. When Mark Twain came to Edinburgh, to escape from the fatigue of being lionised in London, and so that his delicate wife could receive treatment in a famous medical city, he and his little daughter, Susie Clemens, enjoyed the company of that gentle healer, Dr John Brown, author of *Rab and his Friends*. Before he left Edinburgh for home the American humorist, in a spontaneous gesture of friendship, instructed the good physician in the art of retailing one of his famous anecdotes. Mark Twain reported sadly that although John Brown became word perfect in the telling he was quite unable to assume those humorous facial expressions essential for extracting the maximum of mirth from an audience.

I live in an old house in Edinburgh once inhabited by a rumbustious painter from Cumberland, Sam Bough, RSA. Robert Louis Stevenson was a friend of Sam Bough and I believe that he visited the artist from whose house could be caught then, as now, a glimpse of the Pentland hills which RLS so dearly loved. Let the last words come from the exiled Scot who died in Samoa:

> *Blows the wind to-day, and the sun and the rain are flying,*
> *Blows the wind on the moors to-day and now,*
> *Where about the graves of the martyrs the whaups are crying,*
> *My heart remembers how!*

The Plates

River Dochart, Killin

There are those who insist, despite fierce partisanship elsewhere, that Perthshire, which does not touch the sea, is supreme among the Scottish counties. When faced with a composition, like that reproduced in the photograph, it would be hard not to grant Perthshire, at least, the status of *primus inter pares*.

The joyous, tumbling waters of the river Dochart sweep in a flurry of silver spray, between tree girt islands, on their way to join forces with the Lochay, before demurely and sedately flowing into Loch Tay. Looming distantly over the rushing cascades is Ben More, not far from Crianlarich.

Near the bridge, overlooking this scene, almost Japanese in its delicacy of subject and design, is a small island called Inch Buie, which was the burial place of the MacNabs, a notable Perthshire clan. Killin, an unpretentious and attractive little town, is on the fringes of a large area of Perthshire known as Breadalbane, the highest point of which is Ben Lawers, (3,984 feet), eight or nine miles to the east of Killin, on the north side of Loch Tay. The Lawers region, which has recently been equipped with a cleverly designed mountain information centre, just off the well-surfaced hill road leading up to Lochan na Lairige, at the crest of the pass between Ben Lawers and Tarmachan, is celebrated for its profusion of botanical species.

Inveraray Castle

Although there may be a hint of the French *château* about it the massive solidity of Inverary Castle, (modernised and redecorated by the fifth Duke of Argyll, when he was Marquess of Lorne, in the latter part of the eighteenth century), is an early tribute to the neo-Scottish baronial style of architecture. Impressive it is, with its immensely virile yet elegant square-cut jib, the lord of all it surveys, imperiously dominating the land of Lorne, the nearby, romantic town of Inveraray, the green hills of Argyll, and the blue waters of Loch Fyne.

The castle is the hereditary home of the head of Clan Campbell, of the awesome Mac Cailein Mor himself. So powerful is the magnetic field generated by this patrician house that one cannot contemplate its four rounded corner towers with their conical hats (especially if the Duke's personal standard is proudly flying) without being conscious of the part played by the Campbells in shaping Scottish destiny. One's mind is stirred by thoughts of the Argyll of covenanting days and his cavalier adversary, the great Montrose.

If externally this battleship of a castle sends its bow waves crashing through the imagination, its interior and its muniment room provide a rich and lively museum of Scottish history. The treasures of the Campbells provide a heady banquet for the visitor aware of Scotland's often tumultuous past. There has been a strain of wilful if amiable eccentricity about some of the Campbells whose home has been the castle, an aristocratic and endearing indulgence in private whim or caprice, which, even in this age of dull equality, still faintly pervades the atmosphere.

34

Bottom End of Loch Lomond

The pleasure craft are moored close to the centre of the Dunbartonshire town of Balloch, near the point at which the river Leven issues from the southern end of Loch Lomond, to flow through the populous Vale of Leven, on its short journey to join the Clyde. Such, at times, is the throng of boats at Balloch that the view of the river is all but blocked.

Sailing on Loch Lomond, which, 24 miles in length, is the longest stretch of inland water in the UK, is becoming increasingly popular. The marina, on the west side, has become an established institution and on a sunny summer Sunday afternoon, the Sabbath calm can be broken by the zoom of power boats skimming over the waters.

Balloch, a busy but not conspicuously distinguished town, is the home port of the *Queen of the Loch*, the paddle steamer which, in the season, cruises to Ardlui, at the top end of the loch. Frequently threatened with a forcible demise, the *Queen of the Loch* serenely survives, to give pleasure to thousands of tourists decanted at the Balloch pier by 'Blue line' electric trains from Glasgow. As part of her complement she carries, every summer, a young lady purserette, selected, after keen competition, to play the role of Maid of the Loch.

Just outside the range of the camera is the cluster of islands, about 30 in all, which, some of them embowered in trees, add to the enchantment of the southern end of the loch. Ben Lomond, that friendly mountain which presides so benignly over the loch, faces, diagonally, across the waters, Tarbet, a port of call for the *Queen of the Loch*, which is about 16 miles from Balloch, on the western shore.

36

(Overleaf) Gruinard Bay

There are those who regard Gruinard Bay as the nearest thing to perfection on the West Highland coast. Although greatly improved road surfaces have made it much more accessible than it once was it is still a place of solitude.

Probably derived from an Old Norse source the name means a green, or alternatively, a shallow inlet of the sea. The bay is about five miles across and within its outstretched arms lies Gruinard Island which, because of war-time experiments, is still polluted. Access to it is forbidden. It is saddening to come across this grim reminder amidst such loveliness.

There is an oasis quality about Gruinard Bay. For a few miles the road from Loch Ewe to Little Loch Broom passes through a countryside of rich green machair, or turf, of trees, of gentle streams and waterfalls, of glorious white beaches lapped by a sea of lapis lazuli. All around the great, bare mountains of Wester Ross rise up from the wild and desolate moors, studded with little lochans, but Gruinard Bay has the appeal of a garden in the wilderness.

The approach from Loch Ewe used to involve a sudden and dramatic plunge down to the sea shore but vast improvements in the road have blunted the thrill of the descent to the bay. The photograph has been taken from Achgarve, on the west side of the bay, looking towards the splendid tops of An Teallach, the lofty ridge which dominates this corner of Ross-shire. Not far from Achgarve is a tiny township rejoicing in the name of Mellon Udrigle, reminiscent of the Isles of Greece. Highland place names are a constant source of interest. Nestling on the fringes of the bay are two diminutive positions called First Coast and Second Coast.

Highland Piper

The art of playing the bagpipes, as is well illustrated in the study of Piper Serjeant J. Wilson, of the KOSB, calls for concentration, sound lung capacity, and subtle fingering. It is in the strict sense of the word a regimental skill.

There are those who affect to believe that the sound of the pipes is tolerable only when heard out of doors, and at a distance. This is nonsense, but there is undoubtedly something sweetly moving about hearing the pipes played by some invisible piper in a setting of mountain or forest.

The pipes have a universal and an irresistible appeal which springs from something much deeper than their association with battle. Some years ago when it was announced that a thousand pipers would march along Princes Street, Edinburgh, so dense was the throng which gathered along the famous street that the event had to be cancelled.

The pipes stir the blood of every Scot and it is not surprising that Scots of all ranks, from ploughboy to ambassador, take pride in their mastery. They can claim an aristocratic status within the community of musical instruments. To be able to play the pipes competently places one within an exclusive sodality. In cities like Glasgow and Edinburgh the *maestri* of the bagpipes regularly meet to hold what in less patrician circles would be called 'jam sessions'. Classicists of bagpipe music and bagpipe performance are apt to dispute in a recondite manner over the primacy of different schools of piping and pibroch, but there seems to be no doubt that the original Lyceum, in the Aristotelian sense, of bagpiping was located in the tiny township of Boreraig in Duirinish, on the north-west coast of Skye.

42

Abbotsford, Roxburghshire

Still occupied by members of the Scott family, Abbotsford was the last home of the Wizard of the North. Although, since the abandonment of the Waverley railway line, crowds of Americans no longer are deposited by train at Melrose to pay their respects to a writer who was idolised in their country, visitors still swarm, by car, by coach, and on foot to inspect the treasures and relics preserved at Abbotsford.

Through the kindness of Mrs Patricia Maxwell-Scott and her sister, members of the Sir Walter Scott Club of Edinburgh have been entertained, on summer evenings, at Abbotsford, when recitals in verse and song from Scott's works, must have gratified the first owner's shade.

Situated between Melrose and Selkirk, close to the Tweed, Abbotsford may not be the most handsome of country mansions but it fulfilled one of Scott's dearest ambitions, to have a home in the countryside which he loved, and which would provide a worthy repository for all the treasures which he had collected. Scott was something of a romantic magpie and he accumulated, in his life-time, a vast quantity of objects of antiquity, not all of them enthralling.

The Abbotsford of to-day has certainly not been modernised out of existence, although illumination by gas which Scott proudly installed before most of his contemporaries, has been replaced by electricity. The house is largely the same house, inside and out, which Scott designed, in which he lived as a happy country laird, and in which he died. Every room is touched by Scott's breath, and to wander through Abbotsford is to feel close to the presence of a man whose soaring imagination and whose unflagging industry left the world an immortal legacy.

44

Loch Culag and Suilven

Of all the 'loner' mountains which thrust their startling silhouettes up from the geological grand opera which is West Sutherland, Suilven may perhaps be singled out for the status of *prima donna assoluta*. With its twin humps, when seen from afar, Suilven looks like a colossal Bactrian rising from a pedregal of rock and heather.

Although the higher of its two peaks, Caisteal Liath, is only 2,339 feet above sea level the isolation of Suilven and its fantastic contours lend it the aspect of a Matterhorn. Like a lady preening herself before a mirror, Suilven seems to be constantly offering a different profile for judgment. If Suilven is a camel it is a camel with a strong chameleon strain. It has the disconcerting habit of suddenly taking one unawares, of forcing an instant confrontation in the most unlikely circumstances.

Suilven, which means 'eye-like ben', has sometimes been unkindly compared with a sore thumb, a peculiarly insensitive reaction. The profile presented in the plate gives Suilven a patina of repose which is characteristic of its capacity to work a double bluff. It is as if a mountain usually immodest enough to perform a strip-tease had suddenly decided to present a demure and discreet front to the world. Any suggestion that Suilven is naturally diffident would soon disappear if one were to step a few paces to the right or to the left of Loch Culag. The loch lies close to the delightful village of Lochinver, the children of which attend a captivatingly sited school on a little peninsula stretching into Culag's peaceful waters.

46

Sweetheart Abbey

Over the roofs of the snug, whitewashed houses of New Abbey, Kirk-cudbrightshire, the lovely rose window on the wall of the roofless choir of the Abbey of the Sweet Heart, seems to put the relatively new to shame, in contrast to the incontestably old. Sweetheart Abbey, a Cistercian house, was founded in 1273. The warm, red sandstone, out of which it was built, was quarried at prettily named Caerlaverock, across the estuary of the river Nith.

An atmosphere of vernal sweetness seems to pervade those well-preserved remnants of a once bustling holy place, in keeping with its name. If ruined walls can evoke the sentiment of tenderness those of the last pre-Reformation Cistercian house to be built in Scotland do arouse this feeling. There is about this Abbey, dominated by the slopes of Criffel, an aura of gentle, feminine grace, uncharacteristic of its solid, masculine environment.

The Abbey indeed preserves the memory of a lady whose graven image lies within those hallowed walls. The lady founder was Devorgilla, wife of John Balliol, one of the regents of Scotland. John Balliol died before his wife and, until her death, his embalmed heart had been her 'sweet, silent companion'. When the Lady Devorgilla died in 1289 she was buried under the high altar, with the heart of her husband by her side. Seldom has wifely fidelity and devotion been so enduringly and so lovingly commemorated in stone.

48

Loch Hope with Ben Hope

The road westwards from Tongue, after crossing a wild but exhilarating stretch of moorland known as 'A Mhoine', drops down, through trees, to cross the river Hope, where it starts its short journey to the sea, or rather to the wide mouth of Loch Erribol.

To the south lies Loch Hope, a pleasant stretch of water about six miles in length. To the southeast of the upper end of Loch Hope rises the eponymous mountain. If not the most northerly mountain in the UK Ben Hope, a graceful giant, is certainly the most northerly of the mountains over 2,000 feet in height. Ben Hope (3,042) has its supremacy contested by Ben Loyal, to the south of Tongue, deep in the Mackay country, across A Mhoine. Although the main peak of Ben Loyal is only 2,504 feet above sea level its soaring walls look like the flying buttresses of a great cathedral. Those two mountains, expressing optimism and fidelity, because of their relatively isolated positions impart an impressive grandeur to a land of rolling moors which otherwise would be lacking in drama.

From the main road, near the point where it crosses the river, an unpretentious but alluring road accompanies the loch and then, thrusting its modest nose towards the south-east, joins one of the main roads to Lairg at Altnaharra (the burn of the wall). Although merely a glorified track this road is easily driveable. A few miles beyond the end of the loch is a tiny place called Alltnacaillich (the burn of the old woman). At Altnacaillich there is nothing but a house or two, and a forlorn little burial ground. A pause there is mandatory, if only to tilt one's head back to observe a mighty cataract cascading over a lip in one of the ridges of Ben Hope. Sometimes if the upper winds are strong the water presents the phenomenon of 'falling' upwards.

Loch Shiel from Acharacle

Passengers in the tiny vessel *Clanranald*, which, until a few years ago, made daily passage up and down Loch Shiel, from Glenfinnan to Acharacle, embarked on one of the most romantic inland voyages in the world. This long, narrow loch, veering from southwest to west, a few miles from Acharacle, framed by dreamy, 'far shadowy' mountains, their lower slopes green with afforestation, has all the sentimental appeal of a lost cause.

The tall column, at the head of the loch, the Glenfinnan Monument, commemorates the raising, on August 19th, 1745, by the Marquess of Tullibardine, of Prince Charles Edward Stuart's standard, as a rallying point for the clans. Not far from Acharacle, on the shores of the loch, near the green isle which is the burial ground of the Macdonalds, is a little Catholic church, at Dalilea. Acharacle itself is mainly a Protestant community. Glenfinnan at the head of the loch is almost exclusively Catholic. Ecclesiastical relationships between the two villages are of the friendliest, completely devoid of sectarian animosity, a civilised example of mutual tolerance not uncommon in certain parts of the West Highlands and the Isles.

Smothered in rhododendrons, on the ground outside the Catholic church at Glenfinnan, is an old Irish bell. To tap it on a quiet, winter night, with the stars twinkling above the ghostly waters of Loch Shiel, is a moving experience. The slightest touch sends the clear chimes echoing down the mountains, and over the sleeping waters, until, it seems, the joyful tocsin must reach the people of Acharacle, over 20 miles away.

52

Culross, Fife

The photograph, with its glimpse of white-washed walls, cosy, crow-stepped gables, and a rather cheeky little tower in the background, gives a good idea of the intimate, friendly proportions of the unique little Royal burgh of Culross. On the north shore of the Forth, about midway between the Forth and the Kincardine road bridges, Culross offers as compact a survival of early Scottish architecture as is to be found anywhere.

Thanks largely to the zeal and the imagination of the National Trust for Scotland the treasures of Culross have been protected from outrage, and restoration has succeeded in imparting a compelling atmosphere of the past to the little town.

To the right of the photograph, the Study, with its distinctive tower, at the head of Back Causeway, provides a home for the resident representative of the Trust, and contains a collection of furniture, pewter, pottery, illustrating life as it was lived in the sixteenth and seventeenth centuries in Culross.

Culross was lucky enough to be by-passed by the industrial encroachments of the nineteenth century so that many of its early buildings are in an excellent state of preservation. Among them are the Palace, the Ark, and the Nunnery. Some of the old houses have been modernised internally and let to tenants. One of the renovated houses in Culross is Snuff Cottage, built in 1673. It carries the couthy inscription, 'Who would have thought it, noses would have bocht it.'

54

Glencoe, Argyll

The sombre grandeur of this great cleft in the mountains of Lorne can, even on a fine summer day, have a frigorific effect on those sensitive to the evocations of history. The violence that was done on that wintry morning of 13 February 1692, when soldiers, acting under the orders of Campbell of Glen Lyon, set systematically about the massacre of their Macdonald hosts of 12 days, can still chill the blood of an age accustomed to horror.

Although the Macdonalds and the Campbells have, one trusts, long since composed their differences, the atmosphere of Glencoe remains uncompromisingly melodramatic. It seems to have been designed by nature as a setting for tragedy on the grand scale. The tragedies which are now reported, with monotonous regularity from the Glen of Weeping, are not compounded of treachery and clan animosity. The mountains, enclosing and surrounding Glencoe have an irresistible attraction for climbers and every winter the rescue services are called out to search for and succour those who have been injured on the heights, or to bring down the bodies of those who have perished.

The 'new' road (it was built in 1935) which traverses the glen, after soaring sweetly over the desolate altiplano of the Moor of Rannoch, descends, steeply but smoothly, into the eerie defile, flanked to the north by the long, knife-edged ridge of Aonach Aegach and to the south by the three towering Sisters of Glencoe, into the most western of which, Aonach Dubh, is slotted Ossian's Cave. The three Sisters mask all but the summit of Bidean nam Bian (3,766 feet), monarch of the mountains of Argyll. Between the glen and the summit of the Bidean lies a picturesque fold, almost Himalayan in aspect, known as Hanging Valley. The eastern approaches of Glen Coe are guarded by Buchaille Etive Mor (the great shepherd), the dizzy profiles of which are famous among climbers.

(Overleaf) Edinburgh Tattoo

Ever since the Edinburgh International Festival of Music and Drama began in 1947 the Tattoo has been its most popular single event, attracting packed audiences to every performance on the Castle Esplanade. No other military 'entertainment' in the world can be produced in such a superb setting. The Castle itself, bathed in floodlights, or occasionally blacked-out, with a lone piper spot-lighted high on the battlements, provides a spectacular background.

Since its inception the Tattoo has concentrated on the Scottish regiments and on historical episodes relating to the Castle, of which the Army Commander in Scotland is the Governor. But, like the Festival itself, the Tattoo is also international in its scope. Troops from many Commonwealth and overseas countries contribute to the atmosphere of martial pageantry. The audiences are especially responsive to the music: the marching of the massed bands and the production, always entrusted to the military, reflect an effortless precision, which professionals in show-biz might well envy.

One such maestro, the late Mike Todd, was so enraptured by the Tattoo that he expressed a desire to buy it. He did, in fact, arrange to film one performance. Among the many memorable events at the Tattoo was the finale, one year, when Sir Thomas Beecham, wearing a steel helmet, at the request of his anxious wife, conducted the massed bands in a performance of Handel's 'Music for the Royal Fireworks'. In response to his baton cannon from the castle thundered smoke-wreathed salvoes in a *fortissimo* climax.

59

Eildon Hills from Scott's View

The haunting music of the Borderland finds visual expression in this wonderfully evocative trio of hills. Rising just to the south of Melrose they catch and hold the eye from almost every point in the Scott country, with their conspicuous and gentle contours.

The Eildons, in Roxburghshire, are viewed, in the photograph, from Bemersyde hill, in Berwickshire. Walter Scott never tired of this panorama, and the sight of the Eildons over a well-wooded stretch of countryside through which the river Tweed loops its silver way, was a constant source of inspiration to him. It was he who declared, 'I can stand on the Eildon hills and point out forty-three places famous in war and in verse.'

The spirit of enchantment hovers over the Eildons. They have been linked with Arthurian legend and the tale told by the Wizard of the North, Walter Scott, is that his namesake, and partner in sorcery, Michael Scott, the Border Wizard, was originally responsible for the triple formation of the Eildons. Uncomfortable at the spectacle of a demon with nothing particular to do the Border Wizard set him to building a dam across the Tweed at Kelso, to spin ropes out of sea sand, and to split the single summit of the Eildons into three.

On the eastern side of the Eildons is to be found the Eildon Tree Stone which, according to Border folklore, marks the point where, having made a compact with the Queen of the Faeries, Thomas the Rhymer stepped inside the hill for a seven-year sojourn in fairyland. On the southern slopes of the hills is Eildon Hall, the home of the Earl and Countess of Dalkeith.

62

Eilean Donan Castle

If it cannot claim, like those romantic keeps, Castle Stalker in Appin and Kiessimul Castle in Barra, to be built on off-shore islands, Eilean Donan castle surrenders its total insularity only to the point of being connected to the shore of Loch Duich by a causeway.

Eilean Donan is gloriously endowed with environment. Solidly ensconced on its rocky foundation it marks the confluence of three magnificent sea lochs, Loch Duich, Loch Alsh, and Loch Long. Now restored and habitable the castle is seen against the wooded slopes rising above Totaig on the other side of Loch Duich.

Associated with the Clans Mackenzie and Macrae the castle was bombarded virtually to destruction by three English men of war, in 1719, when occupied mainly by Spanish auxiliaries serving the Jacobite cause. (It is of meteorological, if not of great historical interest to recall that at the battle of Glenshiel, fought on 11 June 1718, not many miles from Eilean Donan, a Spanish soldier died of heat stroke.) The castle was extensively restored in 1932.

Until a few years ago the main road to Skye from the south, before reaching the village of Dornie, close to Eilean Donan, made a steep, switchback ascent of Keppoch hill. At the crest of the hill it was almost mandatory for the motorist to stop and, from a patch of green turf, drink in the stunning vista of lochs and mountains. From the Keppoch road one caught a breath-taking glimpse of the island castle. Now most motorists take the new water-level road, gouged out of the hillside. From Invergarry, in the Great Glen, the entire road to Kyle of Lochalsh, the portal to Skye, is almost as smooth and cunningly contoured as the proverbial race track, a contrast to the awkward, but endearing, thin and lumpy roads once so ubiquitous in the Highlands.

64

Stonehaven, Kincardineshire

Although a number of line fishermen still work from Stonehaven, the attractive harbour, as is shown in the photograph, is increasingly used by pleasure craft. The main railway line from the south, which swings inland at Montrose, to follow that part of the broad and fertile plain of Strathmore known as the Howe of the Mearns, converges with the main coastal road to Aberdeen, at Stonehaven, about 15 miles south of the granite city.

Stonehaven is the county town of Kincardinshire, or the Mearns, and it adds a pleasant, bustling air to a coast which can suddenly climb from golden, sandy beaches to stern and rugged cliffs. Now unusually well provided with those amenities which contribute to the success of a seaside holiday, Stonehaven succeeds in looking modestly gay without cultivating any of the garish flourishes which vulgarise some ambitious holiday resorts.

Among its historic buildings is the sixteenth-century Tolbooth which once served as a warehouse for an Earl Marischal and is now a Folk Museum. Until 1784 it was used as a prison. Among the prisoners lodged there were three, local Episcopalian clergymen whose incarceration has led to the building becoming something of a shrine among Episcopalians.

Stonehaven lies in the heart of the countryside portrayed in the trilogy of novels written by Lewis Grassic Gibbon, the best known being *Sunset Song*.

66

Marsco and Glas Bheinn Mhor

The symmetrically disposed mountain to the right, in the photograph, is Marsco, one of the lesser peaks in the southern part of the Isle of Skye, but nonetheless, in its sturdy independence, an attractive one. Behind it, and over the bed of the Sligachan river, rises the looming summit (3,044 feet) of Bla Bheinn, or Blaven.

The main Cuillin ridge, out of camera range, to the right of the photograph, sustains its fantastic challenge to the skies in a sweeping crescent, terminating near wild Loch Coruisk. Most of the Cuillin tops carry the honorific, Sgurr. Marsco seems the odd man out, the name suggesting a brand of chocolate or detergent more than something aggressively Gaelic and primeval. It seems to derive from an Old Norse root, meaning 'Wood by the Sea', although it hugs to its shapely bosom no trees, not even a root.

Marsco, when viewed from Sligachan, looks in some ways, despite its 2,414 feet of height, like a well-balanced, dapper, urbane mountain, full of assurance, but rather determined to keep its distance from the big, arrogant, aggressive Cuillin to the west. To the north of Marsco are grouped the hills of Lord Macdonald's Forest, while to the east, near Broadford, the smooth, pink slopes of the Red Hills of Skye could, compared with the Cuillin, if it is not too disrespectful, pass muster for outsize shale bings.

68

(Overleaf) The Forth Railway Bridge

The mighty spans of the cantilevered Forth Railway Bridge dwarf, in the picture, tiny Inchgarvie, nestling beneath it, in the middle of the firth. Built, between 1883 and 1890, to the design of the engineers Sir John Fowler and Sir Benjamin Baker, this overwhelming yet graceful structure, with a total length of 2,765½ yards, looks indestructible. The hoary tale that no sooner have the painters finished putting a fresh coat on it than they have to start all over again is founded in solid fact.

The bridge, about nine miles to the west of Edinburgh, never fails to impress its invincible majesty on visitors who daily watch, with wonder, the tiny trains crawling to and from Fife. Among those who stared up at its intricate tracery of steel in recent years were that unlikely pair Mr Khrushchev and Mr Bulganin.

On a misty day in 1964 the Queen declared open an impressive rival to the magnificent old bridge. On that day the Forth Road Bridge, slightly up river, welcomed its first traffic. Built to an entirely different design, under the direction of Dr Jack Hamilton, the Road Bridge, an arched structure, supported by cables suspended from two 500 feet towers, has a captivating, aesthetic appeal of its own.

In the photograph the Railway Bridge is seen from the harbour at South Queensferry, a small royal burgh famous in Scottish history. It was at South Queensferry that Queen Margaret embarked on her journeys from Edinburgh to Dunfermline, across the river. Before the Road Bridge was opened countless other travellers negotiated their cars on to the ferry boats for the short passage to North Queensferry. To this day one can enjoy, at South Queensferry, the hospitality of the Hawes Inn, immortalised by Walter Scott in *The Antiquary* and by R. L. Stevenson in *Kidnapped.* On a lesser literary level the Forth Railway Bridge played a part in the filming of John Buchan's *Thirty Nine Steps.*

71

Linlithgow Palace

The old, royal palace of Linlithgow could, with its sylvan and lacustrine setting, be in the heart of the countryside. It happens to be sited not far from the centre of the busy county town of West Lothian, the main street of which is only a stone's throw away from a delightful, civic loch.

The story of the palace goes back to the twelfth century and it intimately concerns the Stuart dynasty. The present edifice was started by James I, and added to by his successors. James V, who greatly interested himself in the architectural design of the palace, was born within its walls. So was his daughter, Mary Queen of Scots. In 1646 the last Scottish Parliament met in the palace.

Over the trees behind the palace may be seen the recently, and in some quarters not too acceptably, erected, gilt 'spire' of the famous church of St Michael's, founded by David I. In one of the two chapels which form part of the church James IV had a premonition, in the form of a vision, of his death at Flodden.

Among the many curiosities in Linlithgow, a town which is balanced between respect for the very new and the very old, is the Cross Well which was erected, from an older design, in 1817. It is equipped with 13 water jets.

74

Tolbooth Tower, Clackmannan

With the wind in the west and the time mid-afternoon the tolbooth tower unpretentiously calls to order the main street of Clackmannan. Accompanying it, as symbols of civic dignity, are the Burgh Cross and Clack-Mannan, or the King's Stone.

County town of the smallest shire in Scotland, Clackmannan has historic links with the Bruce family. It was in Clackmannan mansion-house, no longer in existence that, in 1787, Robert Burns was 'knighted', courtesy the sword of King Robert the Bruce.

There is a tradition that Robert the Bruce erected Clackmannan Tower, which stands on a hill to the west of the town. Clackmannan is skirted by the river Black Devon, which joins the Forth at a point rather ignominiously known as Clackmannan Pow. Pow is the Scottish term for a sluggish stream. To the north the pleasing Ochil Hills rise abruptly above the hillfoot towns of Menstrie, Alva, Tillicoultrie, and Dollar, while a couple of miles to the West is the busy town of Alloa.

76

Traquair House

The fine, old mansion-house of Traquair, thought to be the Tully-Veolan of Walter Scott's *Waverley*, stands close to the village of that name, amid a Peebleshire countryside of quiet valleys, pretty woodland, and friendly hills, a countryside which another Scottish writer, John Buchan, portrayed in some of his novels of adventure.

The house is one of the oldest in Scotland to be continuously inhabited, although extensions have been added throughout its long, romantic history. It was once the home of William the Lion who held court within its walls, in 1209. Among other illustrious figures who 'pernoctated' in it were Mary Queen of Scots and Darnley, in 1566. The great Montrose is also thought to have found a temporary refuge in Traquair House, after the battle of Philiphaugh.

Although open to the public daily during the summer months, the house is famous for a celebrated closure. The gates to the main avenue were closed by the 7th Earl of Traquair, after the death of his wife in 1796. A widely accepted myth, however, if it is one, enthusiastically popularised by that irrepressible romantic, Walter Scott, maintains that they had been closed earlier, in 1745, never to be re-opened until a Stuart once again ascended the throne.

The house contains many objects of historical interest, to kindle the interests of those consumed by a thirst for antiquity. Those with a less exalted kind of thirst may slake it with a taste of the ale from the private brewery established by the present occupant.

Edinburgh Castle and National Gallery

Edinburgh without its castle would still be a beautiful city, but the castle is its crowning glory, the *supremum bonum* with which history has blessed the Scottish capital. With its battlements, bastions, and barracks it imposes itself on the sky-line of central Edinburgh with an authority, civil, military, historic, and poetic. If softened and mellowed this authority is, if anything, strengthened when, after darkness, the castle, on occasions for civic celebration, is illuminated in the glow of floodlights. Seen from Princes Street, in the radiance of the floodlighting, the Castle floats over the city, as ideal, to alter Coleridge, as a painted ship upon a painted ocean.

From the quaint cemetery for soldiers' dogs to the inspiring national shrine to the war dead, designed by the late Sir Robert Lorimer, from the old Parliament Hall to the tiny restored chapel commemorating the saintly Queen Margaret, who died in 1093, the Castle is stored with relics of its stirring past and is the magnet for a ceaseless procession of pilgrims.

The Castle is not so obsessed with the past that it forgets the present. Far from it. A gun, fired from the Half-moon battery, built in 1573, punctually at one o'clock, daily, is synchronised with a ball which is elevated, for the benefit of sailors at sea, on a pole atop the Nelson column on the Calton Hill. From time to time the Parliament, or Banqueting Hall, is used by dignitaries like the Secretary of State for the entertainment of distinguished visitors.

Partly obscured by trees, in the photograph, stands the stately National Gallery of Scotland, housing a permanent collection of famous paintings. Out of the photograph, to the right, is a sister building, the Royal Scottish Academy, the official HQ of Scottish Academicians and Associates which, in addition to housing various collections, holds an Annual Summer Exhibition.

By Little Loch Broom

Lying to the west of Loch Broom, and separated from it by a stretching finger of mountainous terrain, Little Loch Broom may not be one of the most spectacular sea lochs of Wester Ross but it has an appealing charm, testified to by those fortunate enough to spend holidays in the crofting community of Scoraig, which lies on the northern shore, close to its mouth.

The metropolis of the parish of Lochbroom is the little fishing town of Ullapool, on the shore of Loch Broom, about four miles to the east of Little Loch Broom. With its grid-iron pattern of streets, most of them designated in Gaelic as well as in English, Ullapool, a busy place during the holiday months and the centre of an annual, international fishing festival, has an almost Mediterranean aspect.

A rough track over the hills, reached by ferry, connects Ullapool with Little Loch Broom, from which superb views may be had of An Teallach, soaring above the village of Dundonnell, to the south. To the north, about ten miles away, rise the impressive Coigach mountains, the most spectacular of which is Stac Polly which, in silhouette, resembles an upturned boat. Immediately to the north of Little Loch Broom lies the delectable little archipelago bearing the langorous and dreamy appellation of the Summer Isles.

82

Cloch Point Lighthouse

The 76-foot-high lighthouse at Cloch Point in Renfrewshire, on the road between Gourock and Inverkip, with its stubby tower, may lack the lofty elegance of some other beacons, such as the Bell Rock, which protect the Scottish coasts, and it cannot claim the isolation investing some of them.

But to the seamen of the world it must be one of the most familiar of sights. Located at the point where the estuary of the Clyde narrows and turns eastwards towards Glasgow, and facing the green hills of Cowal, Cloch Point lighthouse provides its monitoring and escort service to an enormous variety of vessels, from the famous Clyde paddle steamers to the sinister black Polaris submarines as they surface, inbound to their base at Holy Loch across the water. It is also close to the 'measured mile' where Clyde-built ships are put through their performance tests.

Immediately opposite Cloch Point is the Argyll town of Dunoon, a favourite, among the Clyde resort towns, of Glasgow holiday-makers, a conference centre, and the locus of annual Highland games. Constructed in 1797 the venerable light of Cloch Point shares its navigational duties with a light on the Gantocks, a group of rocks lying just off Dunoon. During the last war a protective boom stretched across the firth, from Cloch Point to the Gantocks.

84

Ayrshire Coast

As the trailer caravans in the photograph indicate, this part of the Ayrshire coast, near Lendalfoot, has a strong appeal for holiday-makers. The shore at this point is strewn with massive rocks, twisted into all kinds of shapes, giving the impression that they had been deposited by some maniacal hurricane far out in the Atlantic. The effect is rather grim and ominous in contrast to the softer vistas to be glimpsed from the road which runs south from Girvan to Ballantrae. The same kind of rock-strewn shore is to be found at parts of the road which skirts the exposed, western shore of the Mull of Kintyre, about 25 miles, as the sea-gull flies, across the wide portal to the estuary of the Firth of Clyde.

The part of Ayrshire which includes Lendalfoot is known as Carrick, and over it broods, or one would like to think, chuckles, the spirit of the immortal Robert Burns. Other authors linked with it are R. L. Stevenson and W. S. Crockett. It is a countryside rich in lore and legend. One of them has it that the lordly occupant of the nearby, now ruined Carleton Castle, having pushed his first seven wives to their destruction, over some cliffs, was himself the victim of a fatal cliff-hanger, the author of his doom being his eighth wife. This part of the coast at one time was favoured by smugglers.

About eight miles out in the firth from Lendalfoot lies the off-shore island of Ailsa Craig, colloquially known as 'Paddy's Milestone'. When seen through a thin curtain of mist Ailsa Craig, a great, roughly circular lump, rising to a height of over 1,100 feet can look like a huge iceberg compounded of granite. The granite is used for the making of curling stones.

86

(Overleaf) Tobermory, Mull

Tobermory, which means the 'Well of Mary', is the capital of the island of Mull. Like Ullapool it was deliberately planned as a fishery centre and, built in crescent formation round a sheltered bay, facing Calve Island and the hills of Morvern, it can boast both an 'up town' and a 'down town' section.

'Down town' Tobermory, with its row of attractive, white fronted buildings, wears an almost metropolitan aspect when one of the red-funnelled island steamers is embarking or disembarking passengers at the pier. One of the hotels facing the water has the rather Nipponese sounding designation of the 'Mishnish'. Mishnish is the name of the north-east part of the island in which Tobermory is located.

With its sheltered anchorage and wooded shore-line Tobermory is a favourite port of call for yachts cruising among the western isles. 'Up town' Tobermory is dominated by the 'Western Isles' hotel, which has established a reputation among tourists. Tourism is now perhaps the chief industry in the island. Among the more recent attractions is one of the smallest theatres in the UK, established in Dervaig, a village a few miles to the north-west of Tobermory.

In 1588 a galleon attached to the Spanish Armada blew up and sank off Tobermory, probably the work of an early Scottish saboteur. Various attempts have been made to salvage the putative treasure aboard this vessel. Although different items, including a cannon, have been retrieved, so far the treasure has eluded interested parties, among whom is the Duke of Argyll.

White Horse Close, Edinburgh

Not so very long ago Edinburgh's 'Royal Mile', sometimes described as 'the bravest street in the world', had degenerated, in parts, almost to the level of a slum. Thanks to an enlightened policy on the part of the city and to the imaginative, sensitive concern of architects, notably the late Robert Hurd, restoration is steadily and quietly being carried out, and already this thoroughfare, leading from a castle to a royal palace, has recovered its dignity, as well as its social prestige.

The Royal Mile consists of three linked sections. From top to bottom, from west to east, from castle to palace, one treads, successively, the Lawnmarket, the High Street, and the Canongate. So drenched in history, romantic, heroic, and grim, is the Royal Mile that the visitor, intent upon making the most of his opportunities, could take a week to exhaust its historical and social repertoire. Fascinating although the frontages may be they provide only the invitation to further revelations within the complex nexus of closes, courtyards, and pends supporting those enticing façades. Almost every yard of the Royal Mile calls for a wondering pause.

White Horse Close, dating from 1623 and restored in 1962, is only one, although certainly one of the most attractive, of the unobtrusive restorations which now reward a passage down, or up, the Royal Mile. Sited on the north side of the Canongate not far from Holyroodhouse, and named after Queen Mary's white palfrey, this courtyard housed the ancient White Horse Inn which figures in Scott's *Waverley*. It was from here that gentlemen set forth on their journeys, by stage-coach, to London. The inn, one of those reserving a room for the use of English gentlemen, was also a well-known haunt for Cavalier officers, and for Highlanders attached to the picaresque court of Charles Edward Stuart.

Glen Etive at Dalness

Homo sapiens must co-exist with the deer in Glen Etive, for there is a little school, not far from Kinlochetive, where the river Etive joins the splendid sea loch of the same name, over the entrance to which that peerless mountain, Cruachan, holds a watching brief. But the modest mansion-house at Dalness is one of the few habitations in this valley of rugged hills and tumbling waterfalls.

The landscape around King's House Inn, near which the road to Loch Etive starts out on its quiet journey to the sea, is so theatrical that as one swings off to the south-west one gets the impression that one is going back-stage. One wants to know what happens behind the Buchaille Etive, with its vertiginous Crowberry Ridge and other challenges to intrepid rock climbers, and what the hinterland to that Wagnerian chorus of *basso-profundo* mountains which throng the stage of the Black Mount, is like.

Glen Etive threads its surprisingly sunny way between the Buchaille and the arrogant peaks of the Black Mount, through what was once a royal forest, with an insouciance untroubled by deferential neurosis. Like Glen Orchy, further to the south, it offers a happy, tranquil escape route, with its green pastures, its singing waters, and its lovely vistas, from a grandeur so wild that it could, at times, become oppressive. In Glen Etive one can recover one's sense of scale, and slowly adjust to the calmer, less turbulent aspects of life.

Plockton, Wester Ross

Seen from near the Bealach nam Bo (the Pass of the Cattle), the 2,054-foot summit on the alpine road twisting through the mountains from Torna-press to Applecross, Plockton is a tiny, dazzling white haven on an inlet of blue Loch Carron, set in a vast amphitheatre of purple mountains, splashed by patches of green forest. Close inspection of the village does not disappoint the connoisseur of the west Highland way of life.

The word *ploc* in Gaelic means a blunt point and the village straggles along the sheltered side of an irregular peninsula facing a steep escarpment on which Duncraig Castle, now a school of domestic husbandry, is perched. There is, or at least there was, a self-contained, independent atmosphere, a life style, about Plockton which reminded one of a Greek city state. Its inhabitants tended to set a clock of their own timing, and it provided the perfect atmosphere in which to hold a Ceilidh which could go on for ever.

In recent years Plockton has been discovered by inquilines from the south, many of whom have established holiday homes in this little paradise of civilised living. Plockton now has its own air-strip. One must hope that urban sophistication has not corroded native conceptions of dignity and comportment. The autochthons of Plockton are all enormously well-educated, in the true sense, and it is not surprising that the recently retired headmaster of the secondary school, Dr Sorley Maclean, is acknowledged to be the finest Gaelic poet of his generation.

One of the great institutions in Plockton is the annual sailing regatta, the atmosphere of which is notably less compromised by protocol than similar events in the Isle of Wight. It used to be a wonderful moment when, at the start of the Ragamuffins' Race (total age of crew not to exceed 21 years), the children hoisted canvas of wondrous design, all of it secretly patched together, with the active connivance of mothers, in the hope of winning the prizes for the most original and attractive sails.

96

Dryburgh Abbey

Although, perhaps, not the most beautiful of the four ruined Border abbeys, Dryburgh could be described as the most affecting. A fragrance of the spirit, comparable to that so often experienced in Iona, seems to settle on those who visit, frequently again and again, this old fane, cradled in a loop of the river Tweed, in a setting of green lawn and stately trees.

Founded in 1150 Dryburgh often suffered the ravages of the military vandal, but the violations of the past are forgotten in the tranquil serenity breathed from those ancient walls. Its St Mary's Aisle, where lie the mortal remains of Sir Walter Scott and Field-Marshal Earl Haig, attract countless pilgrims.

Dryburgh is in the heart of the Border land, which Scott loved and immortalised in his novels and poems, and only a few miles from his home at Abbotsford. It was at Bemersyde, on a hillside close to the Abbey, that the horses drawing the funeral procession paused, at a spot where Scott himself always stopped to refresh his spirit by contemplating the delectable view of the winding Tweed and the enchanting Eildon hills. The visitor to the Abbey, for the first time, could do worse than linger at Bemersyde,(the territorial title of the Haig family), before making his way to Scott's last resting place.

Slioch and Loch Maree

If the day is clear and sunny there are few lovelier vistas in the whole of Scotland than that from the road from Achnasheen to Kinlochewe as it drops down Glen Docherty. Before one stretch the blue waters of Loch Maree, about 12 miles long, with, where it broadens out, towards its north-western end, a cluster of tree-embowered islands.

Framing the loch are some of the most magnificent mountain ridges in the country. To the south, the great, towering Torridon peaks, Beinn Eighe, Liathach, and Beinn Alligin, with their terraced cliffs, quartzite bands, and awe-inspiring corries: to the north, a few miles from the attractive village of Kinlochewe, Slioch.

At times the quartzite on Beinn Eighe looks like snow. The snow on the slopes of Slioch and on the shore of the loch, in the photograph, is obviously genuine. Slioch (3,217 feet), crowns the frontiers of a wilderness of peaks and lochs stretching northwards towards the splendid, crenellated sky-line of An Teallach.

Slioch has a quality of slumbering graciousness compared with the intimidating, if captivating, giants across the loch. Slioch elegantly slumps its massive shoulders in the Highland equivalent of a French shrug. Slioch, although *très formidable*, impresses, edifies, and inspires, and is not alarming.

George Square, Glasgow

Down town Glasgow is being transformed almost out of recognition by soaring, diving, and looping new throughways, but its civic centre, George Square, although picketed by a few lofty 'filing cabinets', as the Rector of Glasgow University derisively dismissed them, retains its atmosphere of solid, spacious dignity.

Crowned by a tower, 240 feet in height, the City Chambers, built in the Italian Renaissance style, impose their florid authority on one of the Glaswegian's favourite arenas. The interior of the City Chambers is laid out and decorated in such a grand manner that newly elected city councillors might entertain the notion that they were conducting their business in some metropolitan opera house.

With its trees and flower beds the square itself affords the citizens an opportunity to take their ease, after the Spanish manner, by patrolling, *en famille*, past the impressive array of statuary, or by contemplating the passing scene from a bench. The tall shaft in the centre, the equivalent of London's Nelson Column, provides an elevated pedestal for Sir Walter Scott. Edinburgh, celebrating him, more extravagantly, or more hideously, according to taste, has seen fit to put him underneath the tributary masonry.

When bands, brass or pipe, play in the square the citizens flock to enjoy the music. In recent years starlings by the thousand have also found the surrounding ledges a favourite resort, and the flutter of their wings during those periodic blitzes is a familiar sound. Various systems of weaponry have been used against those persistent invaders, as well as other ingenious repellents, but, somehow or other, they continue to get through to their target.

Ben Nevis and the Caledonian Canal

The bows of the Rain Goose and the white, toy houses of Banavie frame the colossal, brooding bulk of Ben Nevis in grand perspective. The mountain (4,406 feet) carries its supremacy in the British Isles with a lazy, nonchalant air of contemptuous indolence, like a heavyweight world champion who fears no challenge to his title.

The Nevis massif, with the peaks of the Mamores in attendance like lounging courtiers, is the undisputed monarch of Lochaber and not a year passes without it exacting a toll in human life. Even that mighty Chief, Lochiel, head of the Clan Cameron, whose home is at Achnacarry, not far from Banavie, must occasionally dart a respectful glance at the slumbering giant, across the glen and over the trees. When the snows on its humped summit are flushed with the rays of the setting sun the great Ben, seen from somewhere near Glenfinnan on the road to the isles, takes on a sleepy, ethereal beauty. It seems incongruous that this arrogant mountain, with its stupendous northern cliffs, provides the terrain for an annual footrace to its summit, and that it has been crested by men driving motor cars, and by at least one man, heaving a piano to the top.

Ben Nevis acquires an extra bonus by thrusting its height up virtually from sea level. The Caledonian Canal, an inland waterway of great charm and surprisingly little recognised by addicts of slow and peaceful motion, in its leisurely return to sea level passes through a series of eight locks, known as 'Nepture's Stairway', at Banavie.

(Overleaf) Crail, Fife

With many royal connections the county of Fife is often referred to as 'the Kingdom'. It has also been described, more romantically, as 'a beggar's mantle fringed with gold'. Crail is one of the golden gems on the fringe.

That part of Fife where the hills, in their approach to the sea gently lose height, is known as the East Neuk. In profile Fife bears a resemblance to an Aberdeen terrier's head and Crail comes just under the point of the nose. It is the most easterly of the charming little fishing towns which cluster along the northern shores of the broad estuary of the Forth.

With its picturesque red-tiled, crow-stepped houses, its ancient church, its castle walk, and its fishing harbour, Crail has long been a favourite holiday resort and a haunt for artists. In recent years it has also, during term time, absorbed an overflow of students from St Andrews, which lies about 10 miles along the coast.

Fife is a happy hunting ground for the preservationist, intent on safeguarding its many treasures. Both the National Trust for Scotland and the East Neuk Preservation Trust hold a watching brief over Crail. Recently when the old castle walk fell into a state of disrepair the small local community was able to raise a considerable sum to ensure its restoration.

From Crail one can look across the Forth to the Bass Rock and North Berwick Law in East Lothian. The town also commands a fine view of the Isle of May with its lighthouse and its temptations for ornithologists.

Clath Leathad from the Black Mount

Black Mount is the name given to a lofty, rolling, desolate terrain, stretching from the Moor of Rannoch, in the east, to a towering amphitheatre of swaggering mountains, in the west. This is a bleak, barren country, pitted with lochs and lochans, all of them, like the magnificent peaks, identified by Gaelic names which sound like a roll call of contemptuous giants. The landscape, sculptured with a generous disregard for time or space, is of primitive grandeur.

Northwest from Loch Tulla, near Inveroran, where the bard, Duncan Ban MacIntyre, was born in 1742, the nexus of mountains, many of them, like Clath Leathad, well over 3,000 feet high, present a great, curving barrier to Glen Etive and the peaks of Glencoe. With its stupendous corries and soaring cliffs this mountain massif maintains, unlike the Cairngorm group, a proud seclusion, and an invincible resistance to being tamed by the tourist, or winter sportsman.

The old road over the Black Mount, starting near Inveroran at the west end of Loch Tulla, pursues a western course, closer to the mountains. Between the old road and the track of the West Highland railway the so-called 'new' road sings across the moors, its long, level stretches punctuated by cleverly engineered curves, grades, and bridges. From Bridge of Orchy to Ballachulish it provides possibly the greatest length of virtually 'untenanted' main road in Scotland. On a clear day superb vistas can be had, over the bare Moor of Rannoch, with, far to the east, the slender cone of Schiehallion, in Perthshire, stylishly beckoning.

Dumfries, with Burns statue

The author of that satirical masterpiece, 'Holy Willie's Prayer', might find it incongruous to discover himself commemorated in stone in front of a presbyterian church. But Robert Burns was a man of tolerant disposition and he probably would not regard it as a monumental insult to have himself juxtaposed with the kirk of Greyfriars in the centre of Dumfries, the town with which he was so closely associated, and in which his all-too-short life came to an end in 1796.

The Dumfries church in which Robert Burns had a pew and in which he worshipped was St Michael's. In the churchyard of St Michael's is a mausoleum, in which the poet, his wife, and several children were buried.

Dumfries, a town steeped in historical memories, lies on the river Nith which separates it from its suburb Maxwelltown (in the neighbouring county of Kirkcudbright), the braes of which are, thanks to the bard, perpetually bonnie. Burns did much of his work in Dumfries, and a writer of lesser, but solid, reputation, Sir James Barrie, went to school in the town's Academy. In the year 1306 Scottish destiny was formidably affected when, in the former Greyfriar's Monastery Church, Robert the Bruce stabbed to death the 'Red Comyn'.

Today Dumfries is an important town, the natural centre of a prosperous agricultural area. It may no longer bask in the glory of providing a habitation for a living poet of international fame, but it still serves the purposes of literature by affording space to one of the best bookshops in Scotland.

112

St Andrews Harbour

St Andrews, as the photograph clearly illustrates, is one of those towns in which restoration is achieved in the presence of monuments of the past too ancient to be restored to serve the purposes for which they were originally designed. The pleasant buildings, comfortably situated by the harbour, reveal the hand of the restorer while the tall tower of St Regulus and the lofty ruins of the cathedral relate to a past too venerable to renew.

The pier, in the foreground, thrusts out to a bay, the waters of which can send the waves crashing in through the harbour mouth when storms rage in the North Sea, often drenching the beacon light. The pier, on Sunday mornings during university term, is the scene of a picturesque promenade. After the service at St Salvator's chapel the undergraduates in their scarlet gowns walk to the end of the pier in colourful procession. The more adventurous participants in this academic ritual climb a ladder at the end of the pier and walk back along the top of the elevated retaining wall, running the risk of a splashing on days when heavy seas are running.

To the right of the photograph are the ruins of St Andrews castle, while, also out of sight, are the collegiate and other buildings of Scotland's oldest university, the third oldest in the UK. St Andrews thrives on a mixture of scholarship, golf, and tourism, laced with memories of homiletics and homicide on the grand scale. Every year, in the Spring, the university's Kate Kennedy Club revives an academic story stretching back to 1411 by staging a picaresque procession presenting, in costume, figures from the heroic past.

114

Holyroodhouse, Edinburgh

If the royal palace of Holyroodhouse is much less a place of relaxation for the Sovereign and her family than her other Scottish home at Balmoral its closeness to the green turf of Holyrood park, dominated by Edinburgh's private mountain, Arthur's Seat (822 feet), offers unobtrusive opportunities to shed the cares of State. Those opportunities are regularly taken by members of the Royal family, on foot or on horseback.

The palace garden provides a pleasantly spacious arena for the Royal parties held during the Queen's annual residence, and for that given by her representative, the Lord High Commissioner to the General Assembly of the Church of Scotland, the palace being his official residence during the Assembly. It also serves other purposes, such as providing a landing place for the Duke of Edinburgh's helicopter and a reasonably secluded area in which those ardent toxophilists, the Queen's Bodyguard in Scotland, the Royal Company of Archers, in their picturesque uniforms, can hold some of their shoots, including their periodic contests with their old friends and adversaries, the Woodmen of Arden.

There is a homely, intimate atmosphere about Holyroodhouse despite its suggestion of French elegance. When she is in Holyroodhouse Her Majesty is closer to her immediate neighbours, few of them, if any, aristocratic, than in any of her other Royal homes. Her neighbours, in turn, accept the presence of the people next door calmly, and without fuss, so that, although the ceremonial aspect of Royal visits to Edinburgh is observed with appropriate style and panache, formality at other times is happily kept to a minimum.

With its associations with so many Royal figures of the past, including of course, Mary Queen of Scots, it is not possible here even to offer a brief listing of the events tragic, sombre, gay, and romantic which have taken place in a building which has accommodated so much of Scottish history. One rather quaint and eccentric procedure which, until fairly recently, took place in Holyroodhouse was the election of representative Scottish peers. On the appropriate day the noblemen of Scotland, whose peerages predated the Treaty of Union, would assemble round a green baize table in a room of the palace and solemnly announce their nominees for the House of Lords, more often than not ending with the words, 'And I vote for myself.'

Loch Morlich and the Cairngorms

The shores of Loch Morlich, under the soft, white seal of snow, emphasise that this part of the central Scottish Highlands is now the most intensive centre of winter sports within the UK. With a growing complex of smart hotels at Coylum Bridge and Aviemore, a few miles to the north-west, and the slopes of Cairn Gorm, a mile or two to the southeast, criss-crossed with ski-tows, Glenmore Lodge, close to the loch, forms the lively HQ for all kinds of adventure pursuits, from orienteering and sailing, to climbing and ski-ing. The Grampian hills, where once Norval tended his flocks, now attract sports lovers of all kinds, and not during the winter months only.

If Loch Morlich, in the heart of Rothiemurchus forest, is not quite so romantic as its near neighbour, Loch an Eilean, in its sylvan setting, on a calm day the spectacle of the mountains mirrored in this blue pool with its sandy beach can be enchanting. The four summits of the Cairngorms, Cairn Gorm itself, Ben MacDhui, Cairn Toul and Braeriach, are all over 4,000 feet, the two latter being separated from the two former by the Lairig Ghru, that majestic notch which rises to 2,773 feet at the March burn, near the Pools of Dee.

Too many tragedies have testified to the grim fact that the gales which can suddenly transform the plateau of the Cairngorms into a white hell can create a vicious pattern of weather, at times more brutal in its impact on humans than that prevailing in Arctic regions. Some years ago a successful attempt to introduce reindeer to the forest terrain not far from Loch Morlich was carried out. Despite the throngs which assemble on the ski-slopes the Rothiemurchus area abounds in charming forest trails on which the wayfarer, with an addiction for green lochans and mountain vistas, can find a peace disturbed by nothing more than a fragrant breeze rustling through the pines.

(Overleaf) Tarscavaig, Skye

Tarscavaig is typical of the small, crofting townships scattered through the islands and western Highlands. With each house well separated from its neighbour, the whole community being apparently distributed in a higgledy-piggledy manner, with a glorious disrespect for the planner, it is not surprising that this pattern of domestic disorder has a strong appeal for the landscape painter.

The township, with a population last listed at 36, lies off an adventurous road which twists and climbs through the parish of Sleat, the most southern of the many prongs which Eilean a' Cheo (The Isle of Mists), thrusts into the sea. Compared with the rest of the island Sleat has a gentle aspect and is even, in parts, wooded. This is why Sleat has earned the right to be called 'the garden of Skye'.

The photograph has been taken on one of those days when the isle of mists belies its name. Fortunately there are many such days. Only a few streamers of cloud are hiding the summit slopes of Blaven, a splendid outlier of the Cuillin, across Loch Slapin. Tarscavaig is about half way along the road which, leaving the A851, stretching down the eastern shores of Sleat to the ferry at Armadale, eventually rejoins it about five miles further on, affording, in its erratic progress, a delightful, quadri-lateral tour. From Tarscavaig and other places on the western side of the quadrilateral enchanting views may be had, over the water, of Elgol and the Cuillin range.

St Mary's Abbey Church, Iona

The Celtic crosses seen in front of the restored Abbey on Iona proclaim the unique place that this tiny island, lying to the south-west of Mull, has in the religious history of Scotland. Tradition, of which one need not be sceptical, has it that St Columba first set foot on Scottish soil, 14 centuries ago, in a little bay on the south of the island. For over 30 years after his landing Columba made Iona the base for his Christian missions throughout Scotland.

After the saint's death in A.D.597 the island, the burial place of some early Scottish kings, endured cruel afflictions at the hands of pagan marauders, but, through the vicissitudes of time, Iona has preserved an atmosphere of holiness which has made it, in the eyes of countless people, an island to venerate.

In 1938, the Rev. George MacLeod (now Lord MacLeod of Fiunary), with the blessings of the Church of Scotland, founded his Iona Community on the island. Since then restoration has been energetically pursued, and under the direction of a distinguished Scottish architect, the late Ian Lindsay, much has been accomplished.

An active life, of spiritual dedication, surrounds the Abbey. The Community has aroused the religious enthusiasm of many, especially young people, who find in the island an ideal centre for energetic retreat and communal effort. With its delicate colouring of sea, sand, and machair, with its ancient memories and symbols, Iona seems to instil even in the most restless and critical minds a feeling of tranquillity and reverence. It arouses, as few other places do, among those visiting it for the first time, or again and again, a sense of family, a sense of close kinship with the saints who came marching in so long ago. In Iona even the impassioned unbeliever must find himself contemplating the verities of his credo *sub specie aeternitatis.*

124

By Loch Rannoch

This exquisite arboreal study concentrates on the foreground of a Perthshire scene. Perthshire offers more sylvan vistas than any other Highland county. Seen from the north shore of Loch Rannoch the conical mountain in the distance is Schiehallion, which might possibly claim the status as the Fujiyama of the parish of Fortingall.

Across the water lies the remnant of the Black Wood of Rannoch. About 10 miles long, the loch has its western extremity a few miles from lonely Rannoch Station on the West Highland Railway. The road ends at the station. After that there is nothing but a rough track over the wilderness of heather which, with little lochans, makes up Rannoch Moor. It joins the main Glencoe Road, near King's House inn.

Between the two village schools, at the Kinlochrannoch and the Bridge of Gaur ends of the loch, two other educational establishments have imparted a scholarly panache to Loch Rannoch's southern shore. Recently the University of Stirling established an outpost a few miles east of Bridge of Gaur. Nearer the Kinlochrannoch end, Rannoch School, a boarding school for boys, roughly modelled on Gordonstoun, is rapidly creating an attractive campus around the handsome, white, tree-girt mansion-house of Dall. With enviable opportunities for sailing, for exploring a remote countryside rich in natural treasure, and for community service, the boys at Rannoch have an ideal environment in which to pursue their studies and to develop the spirit of adventure.

126